GETTING TO KNOW THE WORLD'S GREATEST
INVENTORS & SCIENTISTS

ALEXANDER GRAHAM
BELL

Setting the Tone for Communication

WRITTEN AND ILLUSTRATED BY MIKE VENEZIA

GARFIELD COUNTY LIBRARIES
Parachute Branch Library
244 Grand Valley Way
Parachute, CO 81635
(970) 285-9870 – Fax (970) 285-7477
www.gcpld.org

CHILDREN'S PRESS®
AN IMPRINT OF SCHOLASTIC INC.
NEW YORK TORONTO LONDON AUCKLAND SYDNEY
MEXICO CITY NEW DELHI HONG KONG
DANBURY, CONNECTICUT

To Terri Case—for your dedication to teaching the sciences.

Reading Consultant: Nanci R. Vargus, Ed.D., Assistant Professor, School of Education, University of Indianapolis

Content Consultant: Joyce Bedi, Senior Historian, Lemelson Center for the Study of Invention and Innovation, National Museum of American History, Smithsonian Institution

Photographs © 2009: Alamy Images/The Print Collector: 3, 6; AP Images/Halifax Chronicle Herald, Parcs Canada-File: 31; Bridgeman Art Library International Ltd., London/New York: 26 (Alexander Graham Bell in his laboratory, by Dean Cornwell (1892-1960)/Private Collection); Getty Images/Hulton Archive: 30 top left; JupiterImages/Canstock Images, Inc.: 17; Library of Congress: 12 (Alexander Melville Bell), 10, 24 (Gilbert H. Grosvenor Collection), 7; Mary Evans Picture Library: 27; North Wind Picture Archives: 16, 30 top right; Parks Canada/Alexander Graham Bell National Historic Site of Canada: 13, 20, 30 bottom; Photo Researchers, NY/SPL: 25; The Granger Collection, New York: 28; The Image Works/SSPL: 8.

Colorist for illustrations: Andrew Day

Library of Congress Cataloging-in-Publication Data

Venezia, Mike.
  Alexander Graham Bell : setting the tone for communication / written and illustrated by Mike Venezia.
      p. cm. — (Getting to know the world's greatest inventors and scientists)
  Includes index.
  ISBN-13: 978-0-531-14976-8 (lib. bdg.)   978-0-531-22207-2 (pbk.)
  ISBN-10: 0-531-14976-5 (lib. bdg.)   0-531-22207-1 (pbk.)
  1. Bell, Alexander Graham, 1847-1922—Juvenile literature. 2. Inventors—United States—Biography—Juvenile literature. 3. Telephone—United States—History—Juvenile literature. 4. Deaf—Means of communication—Juvenile literature. I. Title. II. Series.

  TK6143.B4V46 2009
  621.385092—dc22
  [B]
                        2008002296

1 2 3 4 5 6 7 8 9 10 R 18 17 16 15 14 13 12 11 10 09

Alexander Graham Bell
as a young man

Alexander Graham Bell was born in Edinburgh, Scotland, in 1847. He is best known for inventing the telephone. Alexander Bell didn't think the telephone was his most important accomplishment, however. He always thought he would be remembered most for teaching **deaf** people to communicate.

Alexander, or Aleck as his friends and family called him, was only twenty-nine years old when he invented the telephone.

He spent the rest of his life experimenting and coming up with lots of other ideas and inventions, too.

The University of Edinburgh in the late 1800s

If you wanted to be an inventor or scientist, like Alexander Graham Bell did, Edinburgh was a great place to grow up. It was the center of education in Scotland. Edinburgh had an important university that attracted excellent teachers and some of the brainiest students from all over the world.

Both Aleck's father and grandfather were teachers. They taught **elocution**. Elocution is the study of speaking well in public. The Bells also helped deaf people and people with speech **disabilities** learn to speak.

Alexander Graham Bell with his father, Professor Alexander Melville Bell

Aleck had a close relationship with his mother, Elizabeth Bell (right).

Aleck was always interested in communication and sound. Not only did he come from a family of speech teachers, but his mother was nearly deaf. Communicating with her was very important to him. While most people shouted into the ear tube she used, Aleck spoke in low tones close to her forehead. He figured she might be able to "hear" the **vibrations** of his voice.

Aleck was fascinated by sound even as a very small child. When he was only three or four, he got lost in a field of wheat. He started listening to the sound the wheat shafts made as they blew in the wind. He wondered if he might be able to hear the wheat growing if he listened carefully enough.

Even though Aleck was super-curious, he didn't do very well in school. His younger brother, Edward, and older brother, Melville (known as Melly), got much better grades. Aleck was more interested in daydreaming. Professor Bell thought Aleck needed to be pushed harder, and decided to send him to London, England, to live and study with Aleck's grandfather. Aleck's father was a serious, no-nonsense teacher, but he was nothing compared to Grandpa Bell.

Aleck's grandfather (right) pushed Aleck to work hard at his studies.

Grandfather Bell got to work right away to make his grandson into a serious student. He insisted Aleck learn proper manners and dress like a gentleman. He forced Aleck to study for hours at a time, especially the science of sound and speech. After one year, fifteen-year-old Alexander Graham Bell returned home a changed person.

Professor Bell was happy with the new Aleck. Now, his son seemed ready to help him teach people with **hearing impairments**. Professor Bell had invented a method to do this. The method was called "visible speech." It broke down words into their simple sounds. Then it used a symbol to stand for each possible sound. By putting together the symbols, deaf people could see how to create words.

Aleck's father taught deaf people to speak using a system he called "visible speech." This visual speech chart shows some of the symbols Professor Bell created to represent sounds.

12

Like his father and grandfather, Alexander Graham Bell developed a lifelong interest in helping people with hearing impairments. Here he is shown later in life, using sign language to communicate with a student who is blind and deaf.

When people are born deaf, it can be hard for them to learn to speak because they have never heard sounds. Visible speech found a way to overcome that. Professor Bell showed deaf people how to use their lips, tongue, teeth, and throat to make different sounds.

To learn more about how the human voice worked, Mr. Bell challenged Aleck and Melly to make a talking machine. Both boys were anxious to show their father they could do it. Aleck and Melly worked for weeks and tried hundreds of experiments before finally getting their talking machine to work. It was made from the voice box of a dead sheep, and it sounded like a small child crying and calling for its mother.

For fun, Aleck and Melly hid their "talking head" and waited to see what neighbors would do when they heard it. Aleck was proud to have invented a machine that worked.

For the next few years, Aleck continued his education. He fooled around with different experiments and began a teaching career. Then, tragedy struck the Bell family. Both of Aleck's brothers came down with a lung disease called **tuberculosis**. There were no medicines at the time to treat the disease, and both of Aleck's brothers died.

After losing two sons to tuberculosis, Aleck's parents wanted to take Aleck away from England's polluted cities.

The Bells moved to Ontario, Canada, hoping the fresh, clean air would improve Aleck's health.

Aleck and his mother and father were heartbroken. Aleck, too, was sickly, and Professor Bell insisted that the family move to Canada. Aleck's parents hoped that leaving the smoky, soot-filled cities of Europe for the clean air of Canada would protect their only surviving son. Luckily, in Canada, Aleck's health soon improved.

A year after the Bell family moved to Canada, 24-year-old Aleck accepted a job in the United States. In 1871, he traveled to Massachusetts to teach at a school for the deaf in Boston. Aleck became a very successful teacher.

As busy as he was, he still found time to experiment and dream of new inventions. One idea Aleck thought about was how to improve the **telegraph**. The telegraph was a fairly new invention. It sent messages across the country in the form of a code of electrical pulses that traveled over copper wires. The problem with telegraphs in the 1870s was that only one message could be sent and received at a time.

Telegraph messages were much faster than mail delivery by horse and wagon. Sometimes, though, telegraph wires could be tied up for hours. Sending a telegraph message was very expensive, too. Aleck knew that anyone who could find a way to send lots of messages over a telegraph line at the same time could make a fortune.

Aleck discussed his ideas about improving the telegraph system with the wealthy fathers of two of his students. Both Thomas Sanders and Gardiner Hubbard liked Aleck's ideas. They agreed to **invest** money to help him develop his ideas. Now Aleck could put most of his time into inventing. He was also able to begin working with an assistant named Thomas Watson.

Thomas Watson (right), a young electrical expert, became an assistant to Alexander Graham Bell in the 1870s.

Thomas was just the person Alexander Graham Bell needed. Thomas had a background in building electrical equipment. Even though Aleck was a genius at coming up with ideas, he didn't know a lot about building or putting electrical systems together.

Hey, Sanders. I just found out Bell is wasting our money trying to invent a telephone!!

Aleck and Thomas worked day and night trying to solve the telegraph problem. Then Aleck became interested in a much more exciting idea. Instead of just sending lots of coded messages at the same time, Aleck thought there might be a way to send the sound of a human voice through telegraph wires!

I can't hear you Hubbard! Why don't you run down to the telegraph office and send me a message!

Aleck began to spend more and more time on his new idea. This didn't make his investors very happy, though. They thought a "talking telegraph," or telephone, was a big waste of time. They demanded that Aleck spend all of his efforts on their original plan.

Aleck was stuck. He was much more interested in working on the telephone idea, but didn't want to disappoint his partners. Aleck especially didn't want to upset Gardiner Hubbard. Aleck found he had fallen in love with Gardiner's daughter, Mabel. Mabel was deaf and had been one of Aleck's students. Later, in 1877, Aleck and Mabel would get married.

Alexander Graham Bell with his wife, Mabel, and their daughters Elsie and Marian

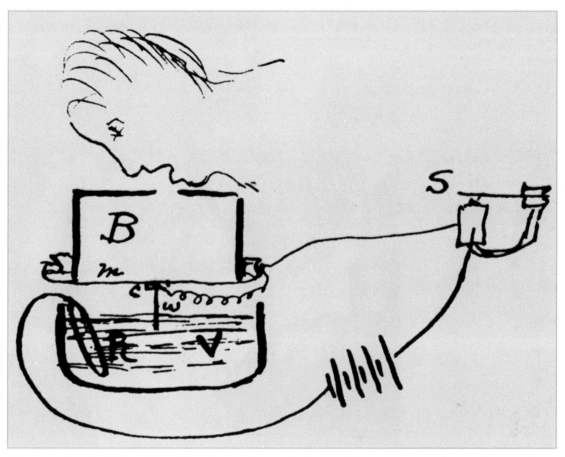

This is a sketch Bell made of his design for a telephone. The invention was made up of a mouthpiece (on the left) and a speaker (on the right).

Aleck decided the only thing he could do now was work longer hours on both projects. After months of experimenting, Aleck's hard work paid off. He had found a way to convert sound into electrical impulses and send them over a copper wire!

An illustration showing Alexander Graham Bell in his laboratory, holding the first version of his telephone

On March 10, 1876, Alexander Graham Bell sent the first telephone message ever. He spoke into the transmitter, or mouthpiece, of his phone, and said "Mr. Watson, come here. I want to see you." Thomas Watson heard the message clearly from another room. Both men were thrilled! They spent the rest of the day celebrating by switching places back and forth trying out the new phone.

Soon Gardiner Hubbard and Thomas Sanders realized the importance of Bell's new invention. They, along with Aleck and Thomas Watson, formed the Bell Telephone Company. Over the next few years, the men worked to improve the telephone's sound quality and to increase the distance that messages could travel.

Bell's invention was a huge success. Before long, cities like New York were filled with crisscrossing telephone wires.

Alexander Graham Bell makes one of the first long-distance telephone calls, from New York to Chicago, in 1892.

Alexander Graham Bell was proud to demonstrate his new invention around the world. It didn't take long before people everywhere wanted telephones for their homes and businesses. One thing, however, almost spoiled Bell's success.

Other inventors had also been working on inventing the telephone at the same time as Bell. But, Bell was the first to obtain a **patent** for his invention so that no one else could copy it. A patent prevents other people from making or selling a person's invention. Several inventors challenged Bell's patents in court and Aleck spent lots of his valuable time defending himself. He never lost one lawsuit, though.

Bell lived a long life. He had plenty of time to experiment with and invent things, like the **metal detector** and the **hydrofoil** boat. He helped make airplanes safer and fly faster. Alexander Graham Bell came up with ideas that were way ahead of their time.

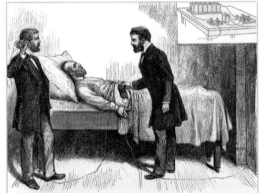

In 1881, an assassin shot President James Garfield. Bell hurriedly invented a metal detector and used it to try to find the bullet. Unfortunately, his efforts were unsuccessful.

Bell was fascinated by tetrahedral cells—frameworks of triangles that are lightweight but strong. In 1909, he tested the *Bell Cygnet II*, a huge tetrahedral kite.

Bell helped develop the hydrofoil, a boat that lifts partially above the water as the boat speeds up. The *HD-4* (right) set a world speed record in 1919.

Alexander Graham Bell
with his grandchildren

Alexander continued working to help deaf people communicate. He was very generous to young scientists and inventors, as well. Aleck opened up a large laboratory and invited inventors to join him. Many of them came up with their own important inventions.

Alexander Graham Bell lived to be seventy-five years old. He died in 1922 at his home in Nova Scotia.

Glossary

deaf (DEF) Unable to hear

disability (diss-uh-BIL-uh-tee) A physical or mental condition that makes it harder for a person to do things that others can do

elocution (el-uh-KYOO-shun) The study and practice of speaking aloud in public

hearing impairment (HIHR-ing im-PAIR-muhnt) The condition of having deafness or poor hearing

hydrofoil (HYE-druh-foil) A boat with ski-like attachments that lift the front of the boat out of the water once the boat is traveling fast

invest (in-VEST) To give money to a project in the belief that you will get money back in the future

metal detector (MET-uhl dee-TEKT-uhr) A device that finds hidden metal objects

patent (PAT-uhnt) A legal document giving an inventor the sole right to manufacture or sell an invention

telegraph (TEL-uh-graf) A system for sending messages over long distances; it uses a code of electrical signals sent by wire or radio

tuberculosis (tu-BUR-kyuh-LOH-siss) A contagious disease that usually affects the lungs

vibration (vye-BRAY-shun) Rapid motion back and forth

Index